The Rosary in Kid Speak

By T.J. Burdick

To all the future Saints this book will inspire, especially Sofía, Saraí, Santiago, and Michael. Call on Our Lady, always.

A special thank you to Mr. Keith Berube, MA, who helped mold this piece of art into a theologically sound form through which Our Lady can be proud of.

The Importance of Praying the Rosary

St. Louis De Montfort tells us in his timeless book on Our Lady, *True Devotion*, that "the safest, easiest, shortest and most perfect way of approaching Jesus is through Mary." The Rosary is the tool that Mary gave to St. Dominic to help us grow in our relationship with her, to recognize her mysterious role in the story of salvation.

In the same way that Jesus came to us through Mary, so do we come to him through her divine intervention as the Mother of all Christians and the Queen of Heaven and Earth. It is through her Rosary that we are tied to God's grace and as faithful benefactors of such blessings, we are better equipped to carry out the personal missions God gives us to complete.

This book was written to help parents complete their mission of raising Christ-like children by helping them come to know, love, and serve Jesus through the love of his Mother. The Rosary, then, becomes the lifeline that unites us with the Holy Family, engaging our hearts and minds with the mysteries that each decade represents.

For each mystery, I have provided two components:

The first is an image of the mystery taken from sacred art over the past two millennia. These serve as a focal point to ignite our imagination and place ourselves in the scene of each mystery.

The second component is a description of each mystery in child-like simplicity. The words were chosen deliberately to identify with children 10 years old and younger so that they can comprehend the basic fruits of each mystery. This will serve as a solid foundation for their faith. As they grow in strength and wisdom, they can be exposed to the sacred scriptures when they are mature enough to understand them.

The Rosary has been called the "epitome of the whole Gospel" (CCC 971) and as such, it teaches children the greatest story ever told. It is recommended that the Rosary be prayed together with your children at a determined time each day so that the seeds of the Rosary can be planted, tilled, watered, and nourished through the repetition, contemplation, and imitation of the virtues it promotes.

How to Pray the Rosary

The structure of the Rosary is as follows:

The Rosary begins on the short strand:

- The sign of the cross on the Crucifix;
- The Apostles' Creed, still on the Crucifix;
- The Lord's Prayer at the first large bead (for the intentions of the pope and the needs of the Church);
- The Hail Mary on each of the next three beads (for the three theological virtues: faith, hope, and charity); and
- The Glory Be on the next large bead.

The praying of the decades then follows, repeating this cycle for each mystery:

- Announce the mystery, then read the Rosary in Kid Speak selection
- The Lord's Prayer on the large bead;
- The Hail Mary on each of the ten adjacent small beads;
- The Glory Be on the space before the next large bead; and the Fatima Prayer to conclude each decade

To conclude:

- Hail, Holy Queen
- The Rosary Prayer
- The sign of the cross.

If you need a reminder on how to pray these prayers, head over to the appendix and you'll find them all there.

Also in the appendix, you'll find a schedule on which days the Church recommends you pray each mystery.

The Joyful Mysteries

The First Joyful Mystery

THE ANNUNCIATION

Fruit of the Mystery: Humility

One day, Mary was praying alone in her room. All of a sudden, the Angel Gabriel appeared and said, "Hail, Mary!" She was afraid at what the Angel told her. The Angel said, "Don't be scared. God has chosen you. You will have a baby who will become the King of the world and you will name him Jesus. The Holy Spirit will come over you and you will become the Mother of God." Mary said, "I am the handmaid of the Lord. I will do whatever God asks of me."

The Second Joyful Mystery

The Visitation

Fruit of the Mystery: Love of Neighbor

When Mary was pregnant with Jesus, she went to visit her cousin, Elizabeth, who was also pregnant. She had the baby John the Baptist in her tummy. When Mary arrived, Elizabeth shouted, "Blessed are thou among women, and blessed is the fruit of thy womb!" This meant that she knew that Jesus was special and that Mary was very blessed to be Jesus' mother. Elizabeth then said, "When I heard your voice, my baby jumped for joy in my tummy!" Mary replied, "My soul brings honor to God. My spirit is so happy because He loves me. He cares so much for those who are poor." Mary stayed with Elizabeth for three months.

The Third Joyful Mystery

The Nativity

Fruit of the Mystery: Poverty, Detachment from the things of the world, Contempt of Riches, Love of the Poor

Mary and Joseph returned to his hometown of Bethlehem. It was a busy time of the year and there was no place for them to stay. Mary was about to have her baby, so Joseph looked for a place for them to stay the night, but all he was able to find was a tiny stable. There, surrounded by animals and the darkness of night, Jesus was born. Shepherds and wise men from far away countries came to visit Jesus and they knelt before him calling him their King. Mary kept all of these memories in her heart while Joseph protected them.

The Fourth Joyful Mystery

The Presentation of Jesus

Fruit of the Mystery: Gift of Wisdom and Purity of mind and body (Obedience)

After Jesus was born, Mary and Joseph took him to the temple to be blessed. Simeon, the priest of the temple, saw Jesus and said, "I have been waiting my entire life to see this boy! God told me that before I died, I would see the King of Kings, and here he is! He will suffer a lot, and so will you Mary, but he will become the ruler of all people in the end." Taking the child and lifting him up toward God, Simeon said, "This is the Messiah, the one you who have sent to save your people."

The Fifth Joyful Mystery

Finding Jesus in the Temple

Fruit of the Mystery: True Conversion (Piety, Joy of Finding Jesus)

When Jesus was twelve, Mary, Joseph, and Jesus were traveling to celebrate Passover. When they began their journey home from Jerusalem, Jesus stayed behind, but he didn't tell his parents. Mary thought Jesus was with Joseph and Joseph thought Jesus was with Mary. After a while, they couldn't find Jesus. With great sorrow, they walked back, hoping they would find him again. When they reached the temple, there he was praying and asking questions of the priests, who were amazed at how smart Jesus was. Mary said, "Why did you leave us?" Jesus said, "Didn't you know that I would be in my Father's house?" Mary kept this memory in her heart. Jesus went back home and was obedient to them.

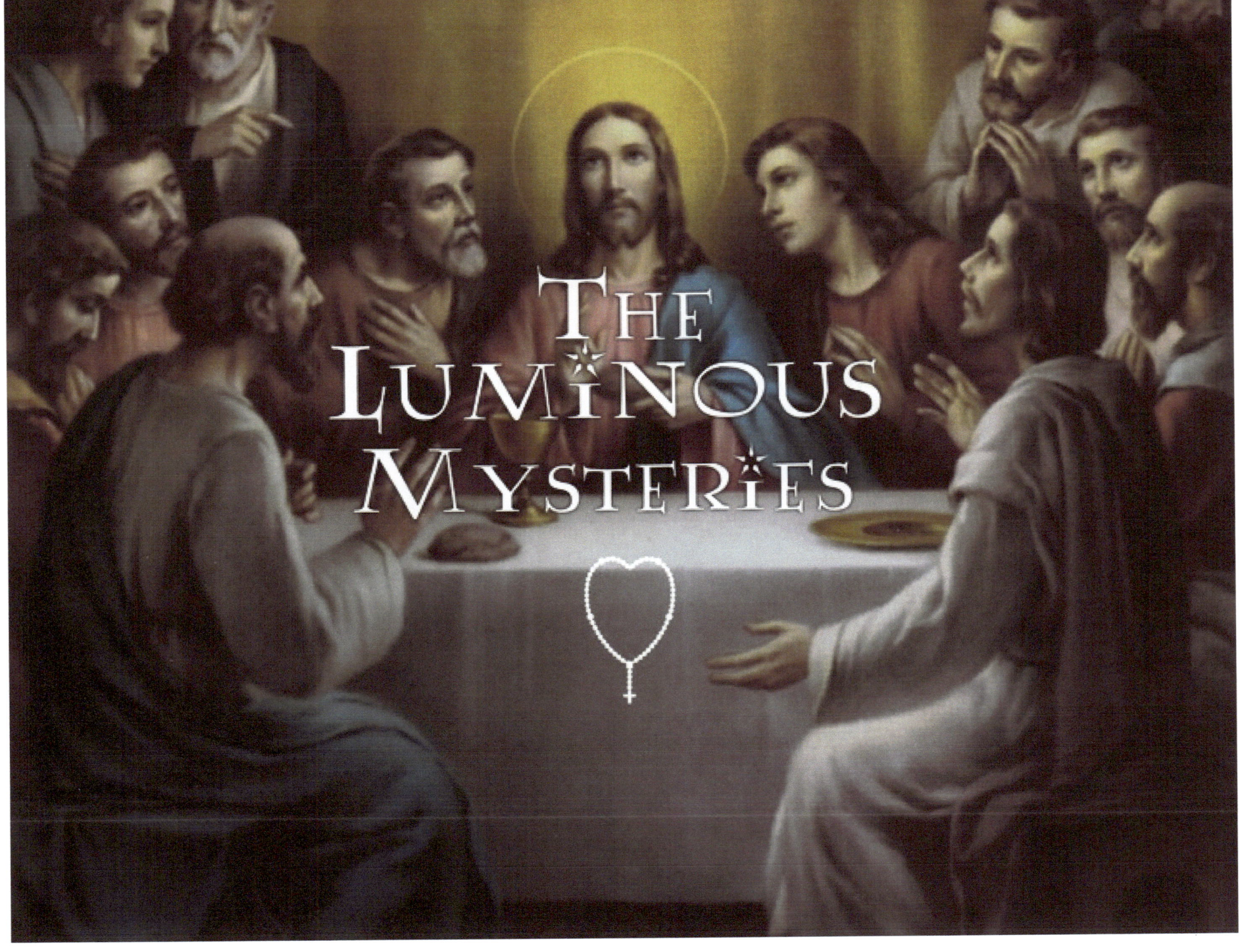

The First Luminous Mystery

The Baptism of Jesus

Fruit of the Mystery: Openness to the Holy Spirit, the Healer.

John the Baptist was baptizing men and women in the Jordan River. These people came to him because they were tired of being sinners. They wanted to be good, so they listened to John's words and repented from their sinful ways. John prepared them for Jesus who would save them from their sins. One day, Jesus came to be baptized by John. When John poured water over his head, the clouds opened and there came a voice from Heaven that said, "This is my Son, with whom I am well pleased."

The Second Luminous Mystery

The Wedding at Cana

Fruit of the Mystery: Loving Jesus through Mary

Jesus and Mary were invited to a wedding. Unfortunately, the party was coming to an end because there wasn't enough wine for the people to drink. Mary took notice, so she did something about it. She called to Jesus and told the people to do whatever he said. Jesus then went to the water jars and turned the water into wine! The people were glad and continued to celebrate with joy and love. This was the first miracle Jesus performed and he would do many more like it throughout his life.

The Third Luminous Mystery

The Proclamation of the Kingdom

Fruit of the Mystery: Trust in God

Since Jesus had performed many miracles and spoke the truth about God, people began to follow him from town to town. They wanted to see him, touch him, and hear what he had to say. One day, he climbed to the top of a hill and told them about the Kingdom of God. He told them what it was like to live a good, happy life, how to love others, and especially how to love God most of all. Because of his words, Jesus' followers grew and grew. Many people began to believe that Jesus was the Messiah, the one who would save them from their sins.

The Fourth Luminous Mystery

The Transfiguration of Jesus

Fruit of the Mystery: Desire for Holiness.

One day, Jesus, Peter, John, and James were walking up a mountain to pray. All of a sudden, the clouds disappeared and Peter, John, and James were blinded by a bright light. Jesus' body began to glow whiter than white. Two prophets who had died a long time ago, Moses and Elijah, stood by his side and began talking with Jesus. Peter wanted to build tents for the three of them, but God interrupted him and said from Heaven, "This is my Son and I am very happy with him. Listen to him." Then, Jesus' body returned to its normal appearance and the prophets disappeared. Jesus told his apostles not to tell anyone about what they saw until after he had risen from the dead.

The Fifth Luminous Mystery

The Institution of the Eucharist

Fruit of the Mystery: Adoration.

The night he was turned over to his enemies, Jesus ate his last supper with his disciples. He took bread, blessed it and gave it to them saying, "This is my Body. Eat it. Do this in memory of me." Then he took the cup of wine, blessed it, and gave it to them saying, "This is my Blood. Drink it. Do this in memory of me." From that day on, the disciples did as Jesus told them. They gathered together to eat his Body and drink his Blood in the Eucharist, which we celebrate every time we go to Mass. The Eucharist is truly Jesus, his Body, Blood, Soul, and Divinity.

The First Sorrowful Mystery

The Agony in the Garden

Fruit of the Mystery: Sorrow for Sin, Uniformity with the Will of God

After Jesus had his last supper with his apostles, he went to pray in the garden. It was nighttime and he was afraid because the next day, he knew he would suffer. He knew that he would die. As he prayed, he begged God to keep him alive, but he promised to do God's will, even if that meant he had to die. He prayed that people would become one in love. When he finished his prayer, soldiers came to take him away and Peter and John, who had fallen asleep, woke up and tried to defend Jesus. Jesus told them to let the soldiers take him away, for it was God's will that he be taken to jail that night.

The Second Sorrowful Mystery

THE SCOURGING AT THE PILLAR

Fruit of the Mystery: Mortification (Purity)

After a long, lonely night in jail, Jesus made the leaders angry because he told them he was a King. Jesus said he was the Son of God, which made the leaders very upset. They wanted to kill Jesus because they didn't want to accept him as their King. So, Jesus was cuffed by his wrists to a large pillar and soldiers whipped him as hard as they could, over and over and over. It hurt a lot. Jesus' body was covered in cuts and bruises and he became very weak.

The Third Sorrowful Mystery

The Crowning of Thorns

Fruit of the Mystery: Contempt of the world (moral courage)

The leaders took Jesus's clothes and made him walk across the room, humiliated. They covered him in a purple robe and they made a crown of long thorns and placed it on his head. They took turns punching him in the face and pressing the thorns down on his skull while they called him names. Jesus remained quiet and never fought back. He chose to suffer because he loved us. When we sin against him, we hurt Jesus just like the people who punched him and made fun of him. But Jesus doesn't punish us back. He forgives us, stays patient, and waits for us to be good. The crown of thorns is a crown of suffering. Jesus is the King of all, especially those who who suffer.

The Fourth Sorrowful Mystery

The Carrying of the Cross

Fruit of the Mystery: Patience

After they crowned Jesus with thorns, they took him into the street and put a large cross beam on his back. He tried to carry the cross through the streets to the top of a big hill, but he was so beaten and bruised that he fell three times. They called another man, Simon, to help Jesus carry the cross. While the two were climbing the hill, Jesus saw the women crying for him. He said, "Do not cry for me. Cry for yourselves and for your children." He knew that we would need his love from Heaven to help us in our times of need.

The Fifth Sorrowful Mystery

The Crucifixion and Death of Jesus

Fruit of the Mystery: Perseverance in faith, grace for a holy death (Forgiveness)

When Jesus reached the top of the hill, the soldiers nailed his hands and feet to the cross. His body was in agony, which means he was in a lot of pain. Many people watched Jesus as he hung on the cross. Most made fun of him. Jesus looked up to the sky and asked God to forgive the people who killed him. Two others were crucified next to Jesus, a bad thief who told Jesus to get him off his cross, and a good thief who asked Jesus to remember him when they died. Jesus told the good thief "You will be in Paradise with me this very day." Soon after, Jesus gave up his spirit, and died.

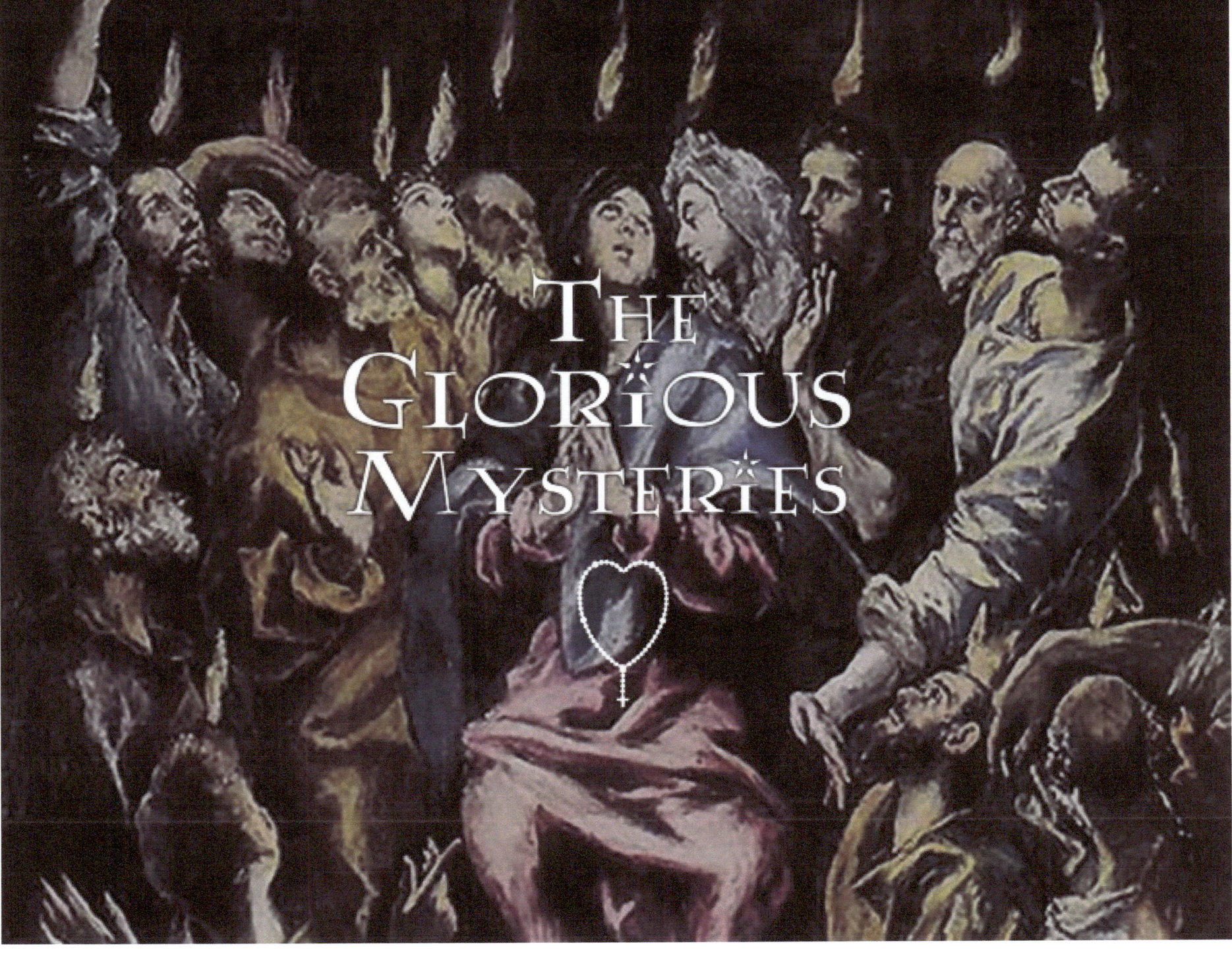

The First Glorious Mystery

The Resurrection of Jesus

Fruit of the Mystery: Faith

When Jesus died, they placed his body in a tomb, which is like a large cave, and rolled a big stone in front of it. Guards kept watch over it because people remembered that he said he would come to life again. Just to be sure, the guards watched. After the third day, Mary Magdalene, one of Jesus' followers, came to check on Jesus' body. When she got there, the stone door was moved and two angels sat in the tomb and asked her why she was crying. She told them she was looking for Jesus. When she turned around she thought she saw the gardener, but when he said her name, she realized it was Jesus alive again! Soon after, Jesus appeared to the disciples. He wasn't a ghost, he was really alive!

The Second Glorious Mystery

The Ascension of Jesus into Heaven

Fruit of the Mystery: Hope, Desire for Heaven

After Jesus came back from the dead, he spent 40 days with his disciples, eating with them, and teaching them about the power of God's love. He told them that there was something more they were going to receive as a gift, but in order to receive it, Jesus would have to go back to Heaven and live there forever. Jesus led them toward a mountain and there he told them they needed to be patient and wait for the Holy Spirit to come to them. He then rose into heaven and a cloud hid him from them.

The Third Glorious Mystery

The Descent of the Holy Spirit

Fruit of the Mystery: Love of God, Holy Wisdom, Divine Charity, Worship of the Holy Spirit

The disciples were gathered together. They locked themselves in a big room because they were afraid the people would hurt them. So, they prayed together for several days. All of a sudden, a mighty wind rushed through the room and tongues of fire began to flame above their heads. They were instantly filled with the Holy Spirit. They went out and Peter, their leader, began speaking to the people about God's love. Everyone who was there spoke a different language and yet, they could all understand Peter. After that day, the disciples were no longer afraid and many people began to follow them. That day is known as Pentecost, the day the Catholic Church was born.

The Fourth Glorious Mystery

The Assumption of the Virgin Mary

Fruit of the Mystery: Grace of a Happy Death and True Devotion towards Mary

Jesus loved his mom very much. Mary, who watched him grow from a child to a man, was his closest and most beloved follower. She was created by him to be a perfect example of love of God and service to others. Because she was without sin and her heart was full of love, Jesus gave her a special gift at the end of her life. Instead of being laid to rest in a grave, he took her body and soul directly to Heaven where she spends eternity at his side. She went to Heaven and is watching over us, protecting us, and helping us come closer to her Son.

The Fifth Glorious Mystery

The Coronation of Mary

Fruit of the Mystery: Perseverance and increase in virtue (Trust in Mary's Intercession)

Since Mary loved everyone so much, she was given an extra special gift when she arrived in Heaven. Jesus crowned her Queen of Heaven and Earth. Jesus, of course, is the King of Heaven and Earth, but Mary sits beside him and helps lead his people by serving them with all of her heart. The Angels, the Saints, and even Mary herself all bow down before God as our one ruler, but we honor Mary as our Queen Mother who guides us closer to Jesus in all that she does.

The Prayers of the Rosary

The Sign of the Cross

In the name of the Father, and of the Son, and of the Holy Spirit. Amen.

The Sign of the Cross is made with the right hand by touching the forehead at the word "Father," the chest at "Son," and the left and right shoulders at "Holy Spirit."

The Apostles' Creed

I believe in God the Father Almighty, Creator of Heaven and earth; and in Jesus Christ, His only Son, our Lord; Who was conceived by the Holy Spirit, born of the Virgin Mary, suffered under Pontius Pilate, was crucified, died and was buried. He descended into Hell; the third day He rose again from the dead; He ascended into Heaven and sits at the right hand of God, the Father Almighty; from thence He shall come to judge the living and the dead. I believe the Holy Spirit, the holy Catholic Church, the communion of saints, the forgiveness of sins, the resurrection of the body, and life everlasting. Amen.

Lord's Prayer (Our Father)

Our Father, Who art in Heaven, hallowed by Thy name, Thy kingdom come; Thy will be done on earth as it is in Heaven. Give us this day our daily bread; and forgive us our trespasses, as we forgive those who trespass against us. And lead us not into temptation; but deliver us from evil. Amen.

Hail Mary

Hail, Mary, full of grace; the Lord is with thee; blessed art thou among women, and blessed is the fruit of thy womb, Jesus. Holy Mary, Mother of God, pray for us sinners, now and at the hour of our death. Amen.

Glory be to the Father

Glory be to the Father, and to the Son, and to the Holy Spirit. As it was in the beginning, is now, and ever shall be, world without end. Amen.

Fatima Prayer

O my Jesus, forgive us our sins, save us from the fires of Hell, and lead all souls to Heaven, especially those most in need of Thy mercy.

Hail, Holy Queen

Hail, holy Queen, Mother of mercy, our life, our sweetness and our hope. To thee do we cry, poor banished children of Eve. To thee to we send up our sighs, mourning and weeping in this valley of tears. Turn, then, most gracious advocate, thine eyes of mercy toward us, and after this, our exile, show unto us the blessed fruit of thy womb, Jesus. O clement, O loving, O sweet Virgin Mary.

Leader. Pray for us, O holy Mother of God.
Response. That we may be made worthy of the promises of Christ.

The Rosary Prayer

The following prayer may be added after the "Hail, Holy Queen":

Let us pray. O God, Whose Only-Begotten Son, by His life, death and resurrection, has purchased for us the rewards of eternal life: grant, we beseech Thee, that by meditating upon these mysteries of the most holy Rosary of the Blessed Virgin Mary, we may imitate what they contain, and obtain what they promise, through the same Christ our Lord. Amen.

The Rosary Schedule

The Luminous Mysteries were included by Pope Saint John Paul II as an optional set of mysteries that may be prayed along with the standard mysteries promulgated by the Church if one desires. Again, they are optional, and can be recited using the schedule in parenthesis as follows:

Sunday - Glorious Mysteries

Monday - Joyful Mysteries

Tuesday - Sorrowful Mysteries

Wednesday - Glorious Mysteries

Thursday - Joyful Mysteries (Luminous Mysteries)

Friday - Sorrowful Mysteries

Saturday - Glorious Mysteries (Joyful Mysteries)

These are adjusted during the seasons of Christmas and Lent.
- *In the Christmas season, the Joyful Mysteries are prayed on Sundays instead of the Glorious Mysteries.*
- *During the season of Lent, the Sorrowful Mysteries are prayed on Sundays instead of the Glorious Mysteries.*

The 15 Promises
for those who recite the Rosary

The following are the 15 promises of Mary to Christians who recite the rosary:
(given to St. Dominic and Blessed Alan)

1. Whoever shall faithfully serve me by the recitation of the rosary, shall receive signs of God's presence.

2. I promise my special protection and the greatest graces to all those who shall recite the rosary.

3. The rosary will be a powerful armor against Hell. It will destroy temptations, decrease sin and defeat heresies.

4. It will cause virtue and good works to flourish; it will obtain for souls the abundant mercy of God; it will withdraw the hearts of men from the love of the world and its vanities, and will lift them to the desire of eternal things. Oh, that souls would sanctify themselves by this means.

5. Those who recommend themselves to me by the recitation of the Rosary shall not die in Hell.

6. Whoever shall recite the rosary devoutly, applying himself to the consideration of its sacred mysteries shall never be conquered by misfortune. God will not chastise him in His justice, he shall not perish by an unprovided death; if he be just, he shall remain in the grace of God, and become worthy of eternal life.

7. Whoever shall have a true devotion for the rosary shall not die without the sacraments of the Church.

8. Those who are faithful to recite the rosary shall have during their life and at their death, the light of God and the plentitude of His graces; at the moment of death they shall participate in the merits of the saints in paradise.

9. I shall deliver from Purgatory those who have been devoted to the rosary.

10. The faithful children of the rosary shall merit a high degree of glory in Heaven.

11. You shall obtain all you ask of me by the recitation of the rosary.

12. All those who propagate the holy rosary shall be aided by me in their necessities.

13. I have obtained from my Divine Son that all the advocates of the rosary shall have for intercessors the entire celestial court during their life and at the hour of death.

14. All who recite the rosary are my sons and daughters, and brothers and sisters of my only son, Jesus Christ.

15. Devotion to my rosary is a great sign of predestination.

The Sacred Art

The Joyful Mysteries

The Annunciation
Perez, Bartolomé M., *The Annunciation*

La Visitation
Ezquerra, Jerónimo, *La Visitación*

The Nativity
Dietrich, Christian Wilhelm Ernst, *Adoration of the Shepherds*

The Presentation
Carracci, Lodovico, *Presentation in the Temple*

The Finding of Jesus in the Temple
Steen, Jan, *12 year Old Jesus in Temple*

The Sorrowful Mysteries

The Agony in the Garden
Van de Velde, Adriaen, *Agony in the Garden*

The Scourging at the Pillar
Bouguereau, William Adolphe, *The Scourging at the Pillar*

The Crowning of Thorns

Bosch, Hieronymus, *The Crowning with Thorns*

Carrying the Cross

Tiepolo, Giovanni Battista, *Christ Carrying the Cross*

The Crucifixion

Lastman, Pieter, *The Crucifixion*

The Glorious Mysteries

The Resurrection
Doré, Gustave, *The Triumph Of Christianity Over Paganism*

The Ascension
Tiepolo, Giovanni Batista, *Ascension*

The Descent of the Holy Spirit
Restout, Jean II, *The Descent of the Holy Spirit*

The Assumption
Le Brun, *L'Assomption de la Vierge*

The Coronation
Velazquez, Diego, *Coronation Of The Virgin*

The Luminous Mysteries

The Baptism of Jesus
Ricci, Sebastiano, *The Baptism of Christ*

The Wedding at Cana
Von Carolsfeld, Julius Schnorr, *The Wedding Feast at Cana*

The Proclamation of the Kingdom
Olrik, Henrik, *Sermon on the Mount*

The Transfiguration
Titian, *The Transfiguration of Christ*

The Last Supper
De Juanes, Juan, *The Last Supper*

For more ways to learn, love, and live the Catholic faith, visit

There, you'll find an easy-to-use Catholic formation curriculum for busy families with young children called *Tiny Thomists*. Each issue includes…

A **"Simplified Summa"** sentence from the *Summa Theologica* to memorize.

A **Lectio Divina** Bible verse to reflect on.

A **Story of a Saint** for each week to ask for their intercession.

A **"Saintly Situation"** to read together that challenges your children to live virtuously.

A **"Read to Me"** story where emerging readers can read the truths of Catholic doctrine to you.

The Gospel in Kid's Speak which is a weekly addition to the *Tiny Thomists* formation program. Now you can read the Sunday Gospel with your young children and they can understand!

On top of these, there will be additional

Family games
Activities
Arts and Crafts Ideas
  and much, much more!

Go to signumdei.com and sign up today.

All images, unless noted otherwise, available in the Public Domain.

ISBN-13: 978-1-950108-05-3
ISBN-10: 1-950108-05-8

Front Cover image credit: Waiting for the Word, *Madonna- Mary and Jesus 38* via Flikr CC: https://www.flickr.com/photos/waitingfortheword/6398398459

www.ingramcontent.com/pod-product-compliance
Lightning Source LLC
Chambersburg PA
CBHW060820090426
42738CB00002B/56